Perspectives on History Series

The Lowell Mill Girls
Life in the Factory
edited by JoAnne B. Weisman

Lowell History at a Glance
by Arthur L. Eno, Jr.

The Mill Girls of Lowell
by Verena Rybicki

A Letter to Hannah
by Shirley Gifford; illustrated by Susan Lippman

The Spirit of Discontent
(from the *Lowell Offering)* by Almira, a Lowell mill girl

Some of the Beauties of Our Factory System - Otherwise, Lowell Slavery
(from *Factory Tract Number 1)* by Amelia [Sargent]

©Discovery Enterprises, Ltd.
Lowell, Massachusetts, 1991

© Discovery Enterprises, Ltd., Lowell, MA 1991
Cover design by Jay Connolly
ISBN 1-878668-06-4

Printed in the U.S.A.
10 9 8 7 6 5 4 3

CONTENTS

Lowell History at a Glance
by Arthur L. Eno, Jr.
Was first published by the *Carlisle Mosquito* under
the headline Lowell History in a Nutshell.
© Carlisle Mosquito, Carlisle, MA

The Mill Girls of Lowell
First American rights, *The Traditional Quilter,*
September and November 1990.
© Verena Rybicki, Lexington, MA 1990

A Letter to Hannah
by Shirley Gifford; illustrated by Susan Lippman
© The Editors, Inc., Lowell, MA 1986

The Spirit of Discontent
Originally printed in the *Lowell Offering*
Reprinted by Lowell 150, Inc., along with a selection
of other articles from the *Lowell Offering* for the Lowell
Sesquicentennial Commission, Lowell, Massachusetts

Some of the Beauties of Our Factory System -
Otherwise, Lowell Slavery
Originally published as part of *Factory Tract Number 1*
by the Female Labor Reform Association, Lowell, MA 1845.
Reprinted by Lowell Publishing Company, Inc. 1982 as *Factory
Life As It Is,* a collection of essays, poetry, and selections
from *Voice of Industry,* November 14, 1845.

Foreword

History can be studied through many sources. Often we rely upon the non-fiction writing of scholars, prepared well after the events they describe have taken place, and presented in textbooks and articles. They are known as secondary sources. To prepare them, scholars rely upon information provided by the people who lived during the time being studied, and contained in their diaries, oral histories, speeches, essays, songs, letters, newspapers, and art. This work, called primary sources, is usually produced by average citizens, and is often the basis for later research by scholars.

Works of art in the form of historical novels, drama, poetry, and short stories can also be primary sources. A fictitious portrayal based on actual events can be presented in many genres—and still convey useful historical content and interpretation.

The following collection of essays and short stories gives the reader a glimpse of life in the factory for the female operatives who worked in the cotton mills of Lowell, Massachusetts in the 1840's.

The book, which contains two primary sources and three secondary sources, begins with a brief introduction to the history of Lowell by Louis Eno. Next there is an overview of the mill girls by Verena Rybicki. The following entry is a fictional account of life in Lowell as seen through the eyes of Adeleen Blake in a letter to her cousin Hannah; it was written by Shirley Gifford and illustrated by Susan Lippman.

Although life as a mill girl had many advantages for the young ladies who came from the surrounding farms and villages of New England, by the mid-1840's many of the mill girls were becoming dissatisfied.

The long hours and poor working conditions were addressed by these young working women in two publications of the day. The *Lowell Offering,* published between 1840 and 1845, was one outlet for expression by the female operatives. The publication contained essays, fiction, and poetry which gave these young women the opportunity to voice their pleasures and concerns about their lives in the factory.

The story entitled *The Spirit of Discontent* by Almira, a Lowell mill girl, illustrates both the benefits and disadvantages of the daily life of the mill girl. Many people outside of the Lowell area were introduced to the life-style of the operatives through this publication.

As conditions in the mills became worse, a stronger voice was heard from Lowell in the form of the *Factory*

Tracts of Lowell's Female Labor Reform Association. One article, attributed to operative Amelia Sargent, was printed as *Factory Tract Number 1,* after having been rejected by the *Lowell Offering* as too controversial. *Some of the Beauties of Our Factory System— Otherwise, Lowell Slavery* is a strong and dramatic call to action for reform in the mills and sets the stage for the women's rights movement in America.

—JoAnne B. Weisman
Lowell, Massachusetts
January 1991

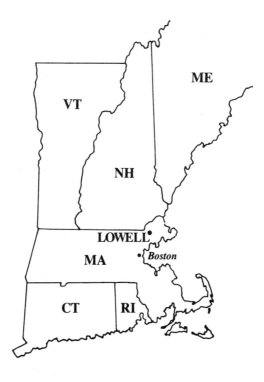

Lowell History at a Glance
by Arthur L. Eno, Jr.

A hundred and seventy-five years ago, the area we now know as Lowell, Massachusetts was a sparsely settled part of Chelmsford. Over 160 years before that it was the site of one of the "praying Indian" villages established by Reverend John Eliot. In 1655, the rest of the area was incorporated as part of the town of Chelmsford. By 1685 newcomers had succeeded in displacing all of the remaining Indians who had not been killed or enslaved during King Philip's War; the survivors sold their interests in the land and retreated to Canada.

Not much happened in the area during the next 125 years, but on the international scene there was developing a movement which was destined to change the world. In Manchester, England, there were the beginnings of the Industrial Revolution. In 1811, a proper Bostonian, Francis Cabot Lowell, sailed to Scotland and England for his health. While in England he visited the mills and was impressed by the power looms in use there. He returned home with the plans for the power loom in his head. Nothing could be written down because English law forbade the exportation of any information concerning the textile industry, and British ships were stopping and searching American vessels for any evidence of industrial spying.

When he returned to Boston, Lowell set about to reinvent the power loom, a task which required, in addition to a prodigious memory, a real mathematical genius. Both of these Lowell possessed, and in a short time the loom was operating (with some improvements over the original British model). Lowell then set up a complete manufacturing operation in Waltham, using the water power of the Charles River; for the first time, the entire process was done on one site: from the cleaning, picking, carding, and weaving, to printing the cotton cloth. The Lowell Manufacturing Company was successful and needed to expand, but the waterpower of the Charles River was not adequate. So Lowell and his partners, the Boston Associates, started a search for a new site with adequate water power. But in 1817, Francis Cabot Lowell suddenly died.

The Boston Associates were led to the Pawtucket Falls of the Merrimack River in Chelmsford and there in 1821 they beheld the thirty-two foot fall of the river. They decided that was the perfect place to establish the projected enlargement of the textile factory. They bought up the land and the shares of the Proprietors of Locks and Canals on the Merrimack River which had already built a small navigation canal around the falls. Then they enlarged and extended the canal, and incorporated the Merrimack Manufacturing Company in 1822. There soon followed seven other cotton manufacturing companies.

The enterprise was hugely successful. Competition sprang up at every waterfall along the New England rivers, and the great need was for workers to run the machines. In a spirit of equal rights and of economy, the millowners selected young New England women to do the work (at a lower rate than would have to be paid to men). In fact, they were more skilled at the work because most of them had been spinning and weaving on hand looms in their farm homes. The recruiting was done by agents who fanned through New England (and later Canada) with "slave wagons" in which they transported the new mill-hands to Lowell. Lowell became a model Industrial city known throughout the United States, and the Lowell mill girls carved their place in history.

Notes referring to this article appear on page 42.

The Mill Girls of Lowell
by Verena Rybicki

Life in the Lowell mills in the 1830's and 40's was hard and most of the mill girls worked there for a limited time only, four or five years, to acquire some financial stability or independence.

The ambition of some of these women was to send money home to help pay farm mortgages or to educate brothers at Harvard. At one time it was said that a quarter of the Harvard student population depended on the financial support from sisters who worked in the mills. Many others were drawn by the delights of city life, the proximity of Boston and the opportunity it would afford them to become women of fashion. One young woman came from the coast of Maine for the libraries, novels unlimited, as many books as her hungry heart desired. And some came for the most pragmatic and feminine reasons: to keep an eye on their beloved who might weaken and take another where the choices were so many, or to set themselves up with a dowry to add to their chances of marrying.

They worked a seventy-three hour week, a total of thirteen or more hours a day, Monday through Friday, with a short eight hour shift on Saturday. In the long mills by the canal, the machines ran for ten to fourteen hours a day. There were as many as 800 to 1,200 machines in a room, all clanging and clanking in unison. The racket must have been deafening. At times, the machines would get into synchronization and this powerful rhythm would start the very building shaking.

Steam was constantly hissing into the room, providing the humidity essential to maintain the correct environment for the spinning and weaving of cotton. Windows were sealed shut to prevent the humidity from escaping, and temperatures would hover between 90 and 115 degrees. The window panes were grimed over by a brown deposit, reducing the light so that kerosene lamps would have to be lit—another smell to add to that of machine oil.

As if the discomforts were not enough, there were accidents to contend with, some of which were sometimes fatal. The huge fly wheel rotated at 75 m.p.h. and if the 900 pound leather belt on it snapped, anyone in line with it was in mortal danger. Shuttles flew across the loom at 90 m.p.h., and if one went astray, it might pierce the brick wall to a depth of six inches. Fingers and thumbs were certainly vulnerable to this onslaught.

Cotton fibers hung heavy in the air along with other pollution, aggravating lungs weakened by tuberculosis or even creating the disease now known colloquially as "brown lung." There was no provision for health care or disability; the injured had to rely on the support of their families, although often their coworkers would contribute.

In the evenings and on Sunday at the end of this harrowing week, the girls were free for other pleasures; that is, as long as they went to church. Regardless of their religious persuasion, Catholic, Unitarian, or Congregationalist, they were required to attend St. Anne's Episcopal Church, built by those proper Bostonian mill owners, who were all pious Episcopalians.

There were many other pleasures: boat trips to Lowell Island for twenty five cents, meals included; a day in Boston by way of the Boston and Lowell Railroad, which was to become the Boston and Maine in 1895; productions of Shakespeare's "Othello"; horticultural shows and concerts. An old music hall bill urges the public to hear "Blind Tom, the negro boy pianist."

Improvement of the mind was of crucial importance and highly valued. The mill girls could attend the Lyceum lecture series and might listen to Ralph Waldo Emerson, philosopher; Horace Greeley, educator; or Professor Peabody from Harvard University. Professor Peabody was most impressed by the determination of the young ladies to learn. There were circulating libraries where they could read as many books as they liked for a membership fee of twenty cents a month (sometimes they charged more for new novels.)

A number of magazines were started to publish the writing of the mill girls. In the initial phases, this drew favorable attention to Lowell, but as conditions worsened and salaries failed to rise, criticism crept into their writing. None of these magazines was sponsored by the mill owners, but they were quick to react to the criticism. Controversy arose among the women about methods of handling the conflict: either actively resisting through "turn outs," as strikes were then called, or, instead, pointing out management's errors in hopes that the problems would be amicably solved.

Of all the magazines, the *Lowell Offering* holds the most prominent place in history. It was published from 1840 to 1845 and fostered three woman who have left their mark on women's history and the textile trade. Lucy Larcom was launched in her career as a poet and writer. She became a lifelong friend of Harriet Hanson Robinson, who later turned her attention to women's suffrage and the abolition of slavery. The third, Sarah Bagley, became a union organizer.

About three percent of the work force in the early days was child labor; in fact, all three of these women started in the mill at the age of ten and continued even after they were absorbed into the adult work force at fifteen. Lucy and Harriet were both bobbin girls or "doffers," a term derived from "doing off," removing the full bobbins from the spinning machines and replacing them with empties. Harriet Robinson has a wonderful chapter about working as a child in her book, *Loom and Spindle.* As she described it, the child's world was not as harsh as the adult's, although children were exposed to the same long hours, heat, noise, and pollution in the work rooms. Fifteen minutes of sustained labor, while the bobbins were being changed, might be followed by forty-five minutes to play or read, particularly if the foreman was kindly.

The mills provided the child worker with three months of mandatory school every year, but the desire for an education was so strong that many of these children attended school voluntarily in the evenings after work. Harriet Hanson had been to school regularly until she was eleven. Wanting to contribute to the family finances, for her mother was a widow with four children to support, she went to work in the mill, but continued to attend evening classes. It is remarkable that she could stay awake for class after getting up at 5:30 a.m. daily. Later in life, she commented that she never made up for that early loss of sleep!

Mrs. Hanson ran a boarding house and Harriet was made much of by the boarders, mainly young men, who treated her exactly like they treated her brothers. Because of their impartiality, she never doubted that boys and girls were equally capable. This must have contributed to her later determination that women, like men, had equal rights and were entitled to vote. She also formed strong bonds with the young women who worked in the mills with her. This led her into trouble, for when they struck over working conditions and wages, eleven-year-old Harriet "turned out" with them. Retribution was swift. Mrs. Hanson was dismissed from her position. It was bad enough that she could not control her boarders, but she was certainly held responsible for the behavior of her own daughter, whose eleven-year-old loyalty to her friends had probably overwhelmed every other thought in her head.

The seeds of destruction of this industrial Eden lay in its success. In the early years, Lowell had become the showplace of American industry and its enormous productivity brought great prosperity. . .and then textile mills with water power began to spring up all over New England. Prices fell because the market was glutted with goods. The mill owners were faced with reducing dividends to shareholders or freezing wages. Not suprisingly, they chose the latter course and the conflict began to escalate. Those New England women had developed a taste for the independence they had acquired through work and were loath to lose it. Publication of their writing taught them that the pen had power, but their efforts to improve working conditions and raise wages led to growing dissatisfaction on both sides and opened the door for cheaper immigrant labor.

By the late 1840's, the New England mill girls were rapidly being replaced by immigrants. The Irish were the first comers, followed by the French Canadians; and after this, there was a steady stream from all over the world that continues to this day and which gives the city the charm of diversity.

The benevolent paternalism of the Lowell mill owners of Massachusetts precluded the disastrous turn of events taken in the textile trade in Europe, where both children and adults were unable to escape from the vicious cycle of poverty and disease. Even so, most of the mill girls were gone by the 1850's and it was not until the Civil War that the ten-hour day was legislated for the Lowell mills.

Conditions grew worse as the century drew to a close. Labor troubles continued into the twentieth century. Eventually, the textile trade of Lowell came to an end, but not without leaving us a rich inheritance in the written records of this time.

A Letter to Hannah

by Shirley Gifford; illustrated by Susan Lippman

March 9, 1840

Dear Cousin Hannah,

Please forgive me for not writing to you since I left home six months ago. Never in my fifteen years has the time seemed to pass so swiftly. Whenever I can, I write to my folks since I am the oldest and the first to leave home to work in the mills.

I feel so proud that I now support myself. I am also able to save money toward my dowry and still have some left for an occasional luxury. I now have a sense of being on my own that I never had on the farm, and as you will see I have learned many things.

You have written that you may soon follow me here to Lowell to work in the mills. I will do my best to describe life in the big city. First, let me tell you of my journey to Lowell last fall. I felt such sadness as the stagecoach came for me early one September morning. My last memory of home is of my family as they stood at the top of the hill and waved goodbye.

As the stagecoach rolled and bumped along through the beautiful New Hampshire countryside, I realized that I really was leaving the farm. This year I would not be growing fruits and vegetables to put in pies or preserves, nor would I be making butter, candles, and soap. My time spent raising and feeding sheep, pigs, and chickens is over for the time being. I am now a mill girl!

The wagon pulled into Lowell after a very long ride. As weary as I was I could only gaze in wonder at what I saw. All the sights and sounds of the city were suddenly surrounding me. There before me were many red brick buildings of three and four floors. Never before had I seen so many people as I did in this city of more than 20,000. Everywhere I looked there were stagecoaches hurrying to and fro, and people rushing about in their fancy clothes. I had never seen or heard so much happening in one place. It was all so exciting!

The wagon stopped before Boott Boardinghouse #52, my new "home". There I was in my plain old calico dress and crimson cloak feeling very forlorn. What a picture I was, clutching my bandbox filled with my possessions, as I fought to hold back the tears. Thank

goodness that I was not alone as there were other girls who shared my situation. Some of the girls spoke with unfamiliar accents indicating that they came from many different parts of New England.

I soon became friends with many of the girls as we shared an eagerness to succeed in our new life. These friendships have made me feel less homesick and have brought me comfort over the past months.

One of the greatest differences between farm-life and factory-life is how our lives are ruled by the bell. I wrote a little poem because it has made such an impression on me. Please do not show it to ANYONE.

The first bell we hear will tell we must,
    Toil all day amid the dust.
The second bell says hurry make haste
    Eat your meals—there is no time to waste.
We wait so long for the bell to say
    Stop your work—you are done for the day.
The last bell signals the curfew hour
    It is time to sleep—goodnight bell tower.

We wake at 4:30 AM to the tolling of the bell. I jump out of my bed, which I share with my friend Sarah Sawyer. There are four of us in one room who must wash, so we take turns using the pitcher and basin. We dress with haste within our crowded conditions. There is barely room for us to move between the beds and the wash stand, with all the trunks and bandboxes stacked against the wall. We quickly fasten our hair up as the bell rings at 4:50 AM, and beckons us to our jobs at the Boott Mill. As I cross the canal to get to

the mill I yearn for my breakfast which will not be served for two more hours.

We must begin work within ten minutes. My job is to tend the loom. This means I must make sure the bobbin is full of thread. If not, I stop the machine, put in a new bobbin, re-thread the shuttle, and then restart the machine. I also must see that the threads on the loom do not break. If one does, I must stop the machine and tie up the broken thread. I am responsible for four looms, but when my friend Sarah is out sick, I mind some of her looms also.

Our wages vary from week to week. We are paid piecework wages, which means the more cloth I produce the more money I make. On the average we earn about $3.50 a week for 72 hours of labor. Out of our wages we pay $1.37 1/2 per week to sleep and eat at the boardinghouse.

Working in the factory means getting used to some unpleasant conditions. The windows in the mill are kept shut so the temperature is extremely warm and

the air is filled with lint. In the beginning I actually felt sick due to the lack of fresh-air. Many of the girls have habitual coughs.

The noise level is so loud that at first I thought I would surely go deaf. By the end of the day I often have a backache, swollen feet, and sore legs from standing so long. My hand and arm hurt too from constantly pulling the lever that starts and stops the machine.

Several weeks ago a girl named Rachel Butterfield was let go. They said her moral character was questionable. She was absent from work too often and made too many mistakes. I felt sorry for her. Even though it is often boring I try to do my very best at my job.

We are required to keep our hair tied up while working in the factory. The importance of this rule was proven last Friday when a mishap occurred. Delia Browne did not fasten her hair up properly, so it became loose and got caught in her loom when she was turning it off. Fortunately, she was not seriously hurt, but it reminded me of how careful I have to be.

We take all of our meals at our boardinghouse. We are given only forty-five minutes to eat dinner and go to and from the mill.

Dinner is served at noontime and is our heartiest meal. Today we had roast chicken and potatoes with gravy, baked salmon, turnips, carrots and onions, pickled tomatoes, corn bread with butter, and bread pudding for dessert with coffee or tea.

There is plenty of food but not enough time to eat it. Often I go back to work with a stomachache.

We still have a long day ahead of us after our noon dinner. We sometimes put up "window gems" to help pass the time. These are newspaper clippings we paste to the sides of windows to read and memorize in our spare time. It is also a common practice to paste poems, hymns or essays to our looms or frames, also for the purpose of memorization. Some of the girls even grow geraniums on our window sills to help brighten the

dreary atmosphere. I do not know how much longer we will be allowed to do these things since the overseers are beginning to complain that these pastimes take our attention away from our work.

The bell tower finally rings 7:00 PM. We have worked thirteen hours and it is now time to leave the mill. As I go out into the cold night air, I can still hear the clatter of the shifting gears and the clanging of the machinery in my head. It almost feels as though I have cotton stuck in my ears. It takes some time to adjust to the stillness of the outside world. I am so relieved as we head to our boardinghouse to have a long awaited supper.

After our supper we have some leisure time. This is when we laugh and talk with our friends, write letters home or sing together at the piano. Here is part of a song we often sing:

When I set out for Lowell
Some factory for to find
I left my native country
And all my friends behind.

But now I am in Lowell
And summon'd by the bell;
I think less of the factory
Than of my native dell.

Refrain:
Then sing hit-re-i-re-a-re-o
Then sing hit-re-i-re-a-re-o

Wednesday is the night of the week we can attend
Lowell Lyceum lectures held in a big room at Lowell
City Hall. The price is $.50 to attend. Many professors
and intellectuals come here to speak. I am looking
forward to a lecture by Oliver Wendell Holmes (the
author of the poem, "Old Ironsides") who is planning
to be here later this month.

Last week a professor from Harvard University
gave a lecture about Ancient Civilizations. It was so
interesting that we all took notes in order to remember
as much as possible. I feel I am learning a great deal
about many different things.

One of my favorite ways to spend my free time is to go shopping. What a feeling it is to buy things with money that I have earned myself. I bought a Highland Plaid Shawl for $1.92, a new pair of shoes for $1.12 1/2 and, my prize possession, a bonnet for $1.50. Sometimes Sarah and I stroll along Merrimac Street arm in arm and window shop. We have such a lovely time figuring how long it will take to save enough for our next purchase.

Religion is as big a part of our lives here as it is at home on the farm. When we begin working at the

mill we are required to sign a "regulation paper" which commits us to regularly attend a church. On the "Sabbath" the streets are full of all the girls dressed in their finest as they come and go from their place of worship.

In Lowell there are many different churches and organized religious societies. I have had the opportunity to try out some other churches and experience their differences. On Sunday I attended St. Anne's Episcopal Church which is the oldest church in Lowell and is quite beautiful.

I look forward to your arrival here in Lowell. I do hope this letter will help you to imagine what your life will be like when you get here. We do work hard and long hours, but that is nothing new to girls like us from the farm.

Our working conditions, however, are less than ideal and it has led to public debate over more than one issue. Some of the operatives (which is what mill workers are called) are trying to get our working day cut to ten hours. They are also asking for better wages, more time for meals, and a healthier working environment. These requests have not yet been answered by the management.

There is also a growing concern over excessive illness among the workers and available health care. The Lowell Corporation Hospital will be opened in several months to respond to the health needs of mill workers.

As you can tell, there are some changes taking place. There are so many new and interesting things to learn about that I have never been sorry I came.

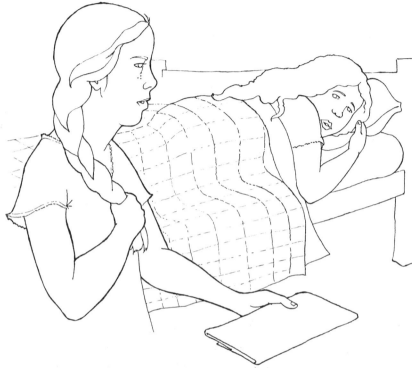

I must close for now as the hour is approaching 10 PM. That is our curfew hour here at the boardinghouse and also when we retire for the night. It seems I no sooner close my eyes when the bell tolls 4:30 AM—time to rise and shine.

I hope this letter finds you happy and healthy. Please write soon.

Your affectionate cousin,

Adeleen Blake

Adeleen Blake

Notes referring to this article appear on page 43.

The Spirit of Discontent

(from the *Lowell Offering*) by Almira, a Lowell mill girl

"I will not stay in Lowell any longer; I am determined
to give my notice this very day," said Ellen Collins, as
the earliest bell was tolling to remind us of the hour
for labor.

"Why, what is the matter, Ellen? It seems to me you
have dreamed out a new idea! Where do you think of
going? and what for?"

"I am going home, where I shall not be obliged
to rise so early in the morning, nor be dragged about
by the ringing of a bell, nor confined in a close noisy
room from morning till night. I will not stay here; I
am determined to go home in a fortnight."

Such was our brief morning's conversation.

In the evening, as I sat alone, reading, my com-
panions having gone out to public lectures or social
meetings, Ellen entered. I saw that she still wore the
same gloomy expression of countenance, which had
been manifested in the morning; and I was disposed
to remove from her mind the evil influence, by a
plain common-sense conversation.

"And so, Ellen," said I, "you think it unpleasant to

rise so early in the morning, and be confined in the noisy mill so many hours during the day. And I think so, too. All this, and much more, is very annoying, no doubt. But we must not forget that there are advantages, as well as disadvantages, in this employment, as in every other. If we expect to find all sun-shine and flowers in any station in life, we shall most surely be disappointed. We are very busily engaged during the day; but then we have the evening to ourselves, with no one to dictate to or control us. I have frequently heard you say that you would not be confined to house-hold duties, and that you disliked the millinery business altogether because you could not have your evenings for leisure. You know that in Lowell we have schools, lectures, and meetings of every description, for moral and intellectual improvement."

"All that is very true," replied Ellen, "but if we were to attend every public institution and every evening school which offers itself for our improve-ment, we might spend every farthing of our earnings, and even more. Then if sickness should overtake us, what are the probable consequences? Here we are, far from kindred and home; and if we have an empty purse, we shall be destitute of *friends* also."

"I do not think so, Ellen. I believe there is no place where there are so many advantages within the reach of the laboring class of people, as exist here; where there is so much equality, so few aristocratic distinctions, and such good fellowship, as may be found in this community. A person has only to be honest, industrious, and moral, to secure the respect of the virtuous and good, though he may not be worth a dollar; while on the other hand, an immoral person, though he should possess wealth, is not respected."

"As to the morality of the place," returned Ellen, "I have no fault to find. I object to the constant hurry of everything. We cannot have time to eat, drink or sleep; we have only thirty minutes, or at most three quarters of an hour, allowed us to go from our work, partake of our food, and return to the noisy clatter of machinery. Up before day, at the clang of the bell—and out of the mill by the clang of the bell—into the mill, and at work, in obedience to that ding-dong of a bell—just as though we were so many living machines. I will give my notice to-morrow: go, I will—I won't stay here and be a white slave."

"Ellen," said I, "do you remember what is said of the bee, that it gathers honey even in a poisonous flower? May we not, in like manner, if our hearts are rightly attuned, find many pleasures connected with our employment? Why is it, then, that you so obstinately look altogether on the dark side of a factory life? I think you thought differently while you were at home, on a visit last summer—for you were glad to come back to the mill, in less than four weeks. Tell me, now —why were you go glad to return to the ringing of the bell, the clatter of the machinery, the early rising, the half-hour dinner, and so on?"

I saw that my discontented friend was not in a humour to give me an answer—and I therefore went on with my talk.

"You are fully aware, Ellen, that a country life does not exclude people from labor—to say nothing of the inferior privileges of attending pubic worship—that people have often to go a distance to meeting of any kind—that books cannot be so easily obtained as they can here—that you cannot always have just such a society as you wish—that you"—

She interrupted me, by saying, "We have no bell, with its everlasting ding-dong."

"What difference does it make," said I, "whether you shall be awaked by a bell, or the noisy bustle of a farm-house? For, you know, farmers are generally up as early in the morning as we are obliged to rise."

"But then," said Ellen, "country people have none of the clattering of machinery constantly dinning in their ears."

"True," I replied, "but they have what is worse—and that is, a dull, lifeless silence around them. The hens may cackle sometimes, and the geese gabble, and the pigs squeal"—

Ellen's hearty laugh interrupted my description—and presently we proceeded, very pleasantly, to compare a country life with a factory life in Lowell. Her scowl of discontent had departed, and she was prepared to consider the subject candidly. We agreed, that since we must work for a living, the mill, all things considered, is the most pleasant, and best calculated to promote our welfare; that we will work diligently during the hours of labor; improve our leisure to the best advantage, in the cultivation of the mind,—hoping thereby not only to increase our own pleasure, but also to add to the happiness of those around us.

ALMIRA

Some of the Beauties of Our Factory System - Otherwise, Lowell Slavery

(from *Factory Tract Number 1*) by Amelia [Sargent]

For the purpose of illustration, let us go with that light-hearted, joyous young girl who is about for the first time to leave the home of her childhood; that home around which clusters so many beautiful and holy associations, pleasant memories, and quiet joys; to leave, too, a mother's cheerful smile, a father's care and protection; and wend her way toward this far famed "city of spindles," this promised land of the imagination, in whose praise she has doubtless heard so much.

Let us trace her progress during her first year's residence, and see whether she indeed realizes those golden prospects which have been held out to her. Follow her now as she enters that large gloomy look-ing building—she is in search of employment, and has been told that she might here obtain an eligible situa-tion. She is sadly wearied with her journey, and withal somewhat annoyed by the noise, confusion, and strange faces all around her. So, after a brief conversation with the overseer, she concludes to accept the first situation which offers; and reserving to herself a sufficient portion of time in which to obtain the necessary rest after her unwonted exertions, and the gratification of a stranger's curiosity regarding the place in which she is now to make her future home, she retires to her boarding house, to arrange matters as much to her mind as may be.

The intervening time passes rapidly away, and she soon finds herself once more within the confines of that close noisy apartment, and is forthwith installed in her new situation—first, however, premising that she has been sent to the Counting-room, and receives therefrom a Regulation paper, containing the rules by which she must be governed while in their employ; and lo! here is the beginning of mischief; for in addition to the tyranous and oppressive rules which meet her astonished eyes, she finds herself compelled to remain for the space of twelve months in the very place she then occupies, however reasonable and just cause of complaint might be hers, or however strong the wish for dismission; thus, in fact, constituting herself a slave, a very slave to the caprices of him for whom she labors. Several incidents coming to the knowledge of the writer, might be somewhat interesting in this connection, as tending to show the prejudicial influence exerted upon the interests of the operative by this unjust requisition. The first is of a lady who has been engaged as an operative for a number of years, and recently entered a weaving room on the Massachusetts Corporation; the overseer having assured her previous to her entrance, that she should realize the sum of $2,25 per week, exclusive of board; which she finding it impossible to do, appealed to the Counting-room for a line enabling her to engage elsewhere, but it was peremptorily refused.

The next is of a more general bearing, concerning quite a number of individuals employed on the Lawrence Corporation, where the owners have recently erected and put in motion a new mill, at the same time stopping one of the old, in which said persons were employed. Now as they did not voluntarily leave their situations, but were discharged therefrom on account of suspension of operations by the company; they had an undoubted right to choose their own place of labor; and as the work in the new mill is vastly more laborious, and the wages less than can be obtained in many parts of the city, they signified their wish to go elsewhere, but are insolently told that they shall labor there or not at all: and will not be released until their year has expired, when if they can *possibly* find *no* further excuse for delay, they *may* deign to bestow upon them what is in common parlance termed, a "regular discharge;" thus enabling them to pass from one prison house to another. Concerning this precious document, it is only necessary to say, that it very precisely reminds one of that which the dealers in human flesh at the South are wont to give and receive as the transfer of one piece of property from one owner to another.

Now, reader, what think you ? is not this the height of the beautiful ? and are not we operatives an ungrateful set of creatures that we do not properly appreciate, and be highly thankful for such unparalleled generosity on the part of our employers!

But to return to our toiling Maiden,—the next beautiful feature which she discovers in this *glorious* system is the long-number of hours which she is obliged to spend in the above named close, unwholesome apartment. It is not enough, that like the poor peasant of Ireland, or the Russian serf who labors from sun to

sun, but during one half of the year, she must still
continue to toil on, long after Nature's lamp has ceas-
ed to lend its aid—nor will even this suffice to satisfy
the grasping avarice of her employer; for she is also
through the winter months required to rise, partake of
her morning meal, and be at her station in the mill,
while the sun is yet sleeping behind the eastern hills;
thus working on an average, at least twelve hours and
three fourths per day, exclusive of the time allotted for
her hasty meals, which is in winter simply one half
hour at noon,—in the spring is allowed the same at
morn, and during the summer is added 15 minutes to
the half hour at noon. Then too, when she is at last
released from her wearisome day's toil, still may she
not depart in peace. No! her footsteps must be dogged
to see that they do not stray beyond the corporation
limits, and she *must*, whether she will or no, be sub-
jected to the manifold inconveniences of a large crowded boarding house, where too, the price paid for her
accommodation is so utterly insignificant, that it will
not ensure to her the common comforts of life; she is
obliged to sleep in a small comfortless, half ventilated
apartment containing some half a dozen occupants
each; but no matter, *she is an operative*—it is all well
enough for her; there is no "abuse" about it; no, indeed; so think our employers,—but do we think so ?
time will show. Here, too, comes up a case which
strikingly illustrates the petty tyranny of the employer.
A little girl, some 12 or 13 years of age, the daughter
of a poor widow, dependent on her daily toil for a live-
lihood, worked on one of the Corporations, boarding
with her mother; who dying left her to the care of an
aunt, residing but a few steps from the Corporation—
but the poor little creature all unqualified as she was,

to provide for her own wants, was *compelled* to leave her home and the motherly care bestowed upon her, and enter one of these same large crowded boarding houses. We do but give the facts in this case and they need no comment for every one *must* see the utter heartlesness which prompted such conduct toward a mere child.

Reader will you pronounce this a mere fancy sketch, written for the sake of effect? It is not so. It is a real picture of "Factory life;" nor is it one half so bad as might truthfully and justly have been drawn. But it has been asked, and doubtless will be again, why, if these evils are so aggravating, have they been so long and so peacefully borne? Ah! and why have they? It is a question well worthy of our consideration, and we would call upon every operative in *our* city, aye, throughout the length and breadth of the land, to awake from the lethargy which has fallen upon them, and assert and maintain their rights. We call upon you for action —*united and immediate action*. But, says one, let us wait till we are stronger. In the language of one of old, we ask, when shall we be stronger? Will it be the next week, or the next year? Will it be when we are reduced to the servile condition of the poor operatives of England? for verily we shall be and that right soon, if matters be suffered to remain as they are. Says another, how shall we act ? we are but one amongst a thousand, what shall we do that our influence may be felt in this vast multitude? We answer, there is in this city an Association called the Female Labor Reform Association, having for its professed object, the amelioration of the condition of the operative. Enrolled up-on its records are the names of five hundred members —come then, and add thereto five hundred or rather

five thousand more, and in the strength of our united
influence we will soon show these *drivelling* cotton
lords, this mushroom aristocracy of New England, who
so arrogantly aspire to lord it over God's heritage, that
our rights cannot be trampled upon with impunity;
that we WILL not longer submit to that arbitrary power
which has for the last ten years been so abundantly
exercised over us.

One word ere we close, to the hardy independent
yeomanry and mechanics, among the Granite Hills
of New Hampshire, the woody forests of Maine, the
cloud capped mountains of Vermont, and the busy,
bustling towns of the old Bay State—ye! who have
daughters and sisters toiling in these sickly prison-
houses which are scattered far and wide over each of
these States, we appeal to *you* for aid in this matter.
Do you ask how that aid can be administered? We
answer through the Ballot Box. Yes! if you have one
spark of sympathy for our condition, carry it *there*,
and see to it that you send to preside in the Councils
of each Commonwealth, men who have hearts as well
as heads, souls as well bodies; men who will watch
zealously over the interests of the laborer in every
department; who will protect him by the strong arm
of the law from the encroachments of arbitrary power;
who will see that he is not deprived of those rights
and privileges which God and Nature have bestowed
upon him—yes,

> From every rolling river,
>   From mountain, vale and plain,
> We call on you to deliver
>   Us, from the tyrant's chain:

And shall we call in vain ? we trust not. More anon.

AMELIA.

Definitions

Bandbox - a lightweight, homemade and rounded box usually made of cardboard and covered with paper; used to hold collars or small articles of clothing

Bobbin - a spool of thread placed in a shuttle

Calico - cotton cloth especially with a colored pattern printed on one side

Dinning - making a deafening noise

Farthing - an early British coin worth one quarter of a penny

Lever - a bar or rod used to run or adjust something

Loom - machine used to weave cloth

Lyceum - an organization which presents or sponsors lectures, concerts and the like

Millinery - relating to the sale of women's hats

Operative - another name for mill girls

Overseer - man in charge of the floor in the mill

Regulation paper - the rules which governed behavior of the employees

Shuttle - a tool in weaving that carries a thread back and forth between the threads that go up and down

Notes

From Lowell History at a Glance

"praying Indian" villages refers to the seven Indian villages where the inhabitants practiced Christianity. Rev. John Eliot and others made annual visits to Indian gatherings in the Merrimack Valley, and converted these Indians between 1648 and 1653.

King Philip's War was the most devasting war in Massachusetts' history. During the struggle for land and power, the English forced the local Wamesit Indians to flee to the woods. They massacred the elderly and the young who remained behind. In 1676 the Indians and local Puritans in the surrounding towns fought many bloody battles, which destroyed hundreds of people on both sides and many local English villages. By the end of all of the devastation, although the losses were tremendous to everyone, the English had taken the land away from the Indians.

Proprietors of Locks and Canals refers to the corporations which bought land in the area to build a transportation system of locks and canals.

In 1792 Dudley Tyng and his associates purchased land to build a canal to bypass the Pawtucket Falls. The Pawtucket Canal, one and one-half miles long, gave the Proprietors valuable water rights.

Soon after, a competing canal, the Middlesex, was built by a rival group called the Proprietors of the Middlesex Canal. These canals, which played a vital role in the early transportation system of Lowell, still exist today.

Notes continued

From A Letter to Hannah

The 1/2 cent referred to was possible because of the existence of the half-cent coin. Half-cent coins were made from 1793 to 1857 and were the lowest valued coin ever issued by the United States. They were discontinued because they became too much of a bother to use. This is what they looked like.

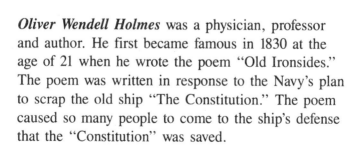

Oliver Wendell Holmes was a physician, professor and author. He first became famous in 1830 at the age of 21 when he wrote the poem "Old Ironsides." The poem was written in response to the Navy's plan to scrap the old ship "The Constitution." The poem caused so many people to come to the ship's defense that the "Constitution" was saved.

"Merrimac" Street has had several spellings over the years. In 1840 it was spelled as it is in the letter. Today it is spelled "Merrimack" Street.

Bibliography

Dublin, Thomas, ed. *Farm To Factory: Women's Letters, 1830-1860.* New York: Columbia University Press, 1981.

Dublin, Thomas. *Women At Work.* New York: Columbia University Press, 1979.

Dunwell, S. *The Run of The Mill.* Boston: David R. Godine, Publisher, 1978.

Eno, Arthur L., Jr., ed. *Cotton Was King: A History of Lowell, Massachusetts.* New Hampshire: New Hampshire Publishing Company, 1976.

Factory Life As It Is, Lowell Publishing Company, Inc., Lowell, MA, 1982.

Foner, Phillip S. *Factory Girl: A Collection of Writings on Life and Struggles in New England Factories of the 1840's.* Urbana, Illinois: University of Illinois Press, 1977.

Josephson, Hannah. *The Golden Threads.* New York: Dueli, Sloane, Pearce, 1949.

Robinson, Harriet Hanson. *Loom And Spindle.* Kailua, Hawaii: Press Pacifica, 1976.

Selden, Bernice. *The Mill Girls.* New York: Atheneum, 1983.

Contributors

JoAnne B. Weisman

JoAnne B. Weisman, editor of this collection, is the president of The Editors, Inc., an advertising agency in Lowell, MA.

Since the formation of the Lowell National Historical Park in 1979, The Editors, Inc. has contributed to the design of brochures, photographs, and articles relating to the history and tourism of the area.

Mrs. Weisman has co-authored, with Kenneth M. Deitch, biographies in the Picture-book Biography Series published by Discovery Enterprises, Ltd. Her books include *Christopher Columbus and the Great Voyage of Discovery* (ISBN 1-878668-00-5) ages 6 - 12; *Dwight D. Eisenhower: Man of Many Hats* (ISBN 1-878668-02-1) ages 11 through adult; and *Leonard Bernstein: America's Maestro,* to be published in July 1991 (ISBN 1-878668-03-X) ages 11 through adult.

Arthur L. Eno, Jr.

Arthur L. Eno, Jr. is a native of Lowell, Massachusetts. He is a graduate of Harvard College and Harvard Law School and has been practicing law in Lowell since 1948. He served as president of the Lowell Historical Society and was the editor of, and contributor to, *Cotton Was King,* the Society's history of Lowell. He was also president and one of the founders of the Middlesex Canal Association and president of the Massachusetts Conveyancers Association. He is now writing a textbook on Massachusetts Real Estate Law for West Publishing Company. He is married and the father of two sons and a daughter.

Verena Rybicki

Verena Rybicki now lives in Lexington, MA, within easy reach of Lowell, but she has always been on the fringes of the textile trade. In India as a child she was surrounded by the brilliance of cotton, and as a teenager in England, her home was near the cotton mills of Lancashire and the woolen mills of Yorkshire. She went to the university briefly in Manchester, England, site of "these dark Satanic Mills" mentioned in William Blake's poem, *Jerusalem.* After emigrating to the United States in the 1950's, she worked as an occupational therapist, a mother, and a teacher. As a writer and quilter, she collects cloth and enjoys exploring the history of spindle and bobbin, needle and thread, and the stories of the people and places behind their use.

Shirley Gifford

Shirley Gifford has a B.A. in English from Boston College. She has experience in editing and as a Secondary English teacher.

A Letter To Hannah is Ms. Gifford's second historical book written for children. *My Colonial Day* (also illustrated by Susan Lippman) was written for second graders and is based on an actual family that lived in a typical Garrison House in 1790 in Chelmsford, Massachusetts.

Both books were inspired by a love and interest in local history and also by the curiosity of her two children, Olivia and Matthew. Nine months were spent researching and writing *A Letter To Hannah* in order to portray an accurate representation of the time.

Ms. Gifford lives with her husband and two children in Danville, CA

Susan Lippman

Susan Lippman has studied art for many years and in many different locations including Pratt Institute and the School of Visual Arts in N.Y.C. and the DeCordova Museum School in Lincoln, MA. She has also studied privately with leading contemporary artists. She has a Masters degree in Education from New York University and is currently teaching in the Lowell public schools.

Jay Connolly

Jay Connolly has studied at Vesper George, Boston University, The Art Institute of Boston, and the Massachusetts College of Art. He served as art director of The Editors, Inc. advertising agency for six years.

In the summer of 1990 Jay completed illustrations for the book *Dwight D. Eisenhower: Man of Many Hats,* published by Discovery Enterprises, Ltd. He is also a fine arts painter affilliated with Lopoukhine Fine Art on Newbury Street, Boston.